FAVOURITE CLASSIC
ARTISTS

LIZ GOGERLY

WAYLAND

© Copyright 2004 Wayland

Editor: Hayley Leach
Design: Peter Bailey for Proof Books
Cover design: Wayland

Published in Great Britain in 2004 by Hodder Wayland,
an imprint of Hodder Children's Books.

This paperback edition published in 2007 by Wayland,
an imprint of Hachette Children's Books.

The right of Liz Gogerly to be identified as the author of the work has
been asserted by her in accordance with the Copyright, Designs and Patents
Act 1988.

British Library Cataloguing in Publication Data
Gogerly, Liz
Favourite classic artists
1. Artists – Biography – Juvenile literature
I. Title
700.9'22

ISBN: 9780750252928

Cover: *The Umbrellas* by Pierre Auguste Renoir

Picture Acknowledgements
Cover National Gallery Collection; By kind permission of the Trustees of the
National Gallery, London/CORBIS; 4 Geoffrey Clements/CORBIS; 6 Francis
G. Mayer/CORBIS; 8 Archivo Iconografico, S.A./CORBIS; 10
Edimédia/CORBIS; Title page and 12 Francis G. Mayer/CORBIS; 14
Bettmann/CORBIS; 16 Francis G. Mayer/CORBIS; 18 Austrian
Archives/CORBIS; 20 Christie's Images/ CORBIS

Printed in China

Hachette Children's Books
338 Euston Road
London NW1 3BH

Terms explained in the glossary have been printed in **bold** throughout the text.

Contents

John Constable   4

Joseph M W Turner   6

Rembrandt   8

Édouard Manet   10

Pierre Auguste Renoir   12

Auguste Rodin   14

Paul Cézanne   16

Gustav Klimt   18

Mary Cassatt   20

Other favourite classic artists   22

Glossary & Index   24

John Constable | 1776-1837

John Constable is the English pioneer of landscape painting. In many of his greatest works he painted nature and the countryside.

Early Years
Born in 1776 in the village of East Bergholt, Suffolk, he was the son of a successful miller. His father hoped his artistic son would follow him into the family business but in 1799 Constable joined the Royal Academy School

The White Horse Of this painting Constable said: [it was] 'one of my happiest efforts on a large scale, being a placid representation of a serene grey morning, summer.'

in London to study art.

Constable exhibited his first work at the Royal Academy in 1802 but it wasn't until the 1820s

'The sound of water escaping from mill-dams, willows, old rotten planks, slimy posts, and brickwork, I love such things…those scenes made me a painter and I am grateful.'

Letter from John Constable to John Fisher, *Memoirs of the Life of John Constable* by C. R. Leslie

that his work was really noticed. Constable's father had died in 1816 and he had inherited enough money to devote himself to his painting and to marry his long-time sweetheart Maria Bicknell. In 1824 his painting, *The Haywain*, won a gold medal award in Paris. The following year he caused another stir with his painting *The White Horse*.

Later Life

Constable moved to Hampstead, London in 1819. In the following years Maria developed tuberculosis and they regularly visited Brighton to take the sea air. Maria died in 1828 and Constable was heartbroken. Many of his paintings after her death reflect his feelings of anger and depression. *Hadleigh Castle* (1829) for example, shows the sunrise after a dark and stormy night that must have reflected Constable's dark mood. At a time when most gentlemen chose to travel throughout Europe Constable always remained in his beloved England. Sadly, in his own lifetime he did not get the recognition or success there that he deserved. Now, his famous landscape paintings, such as *The Cornfield* and *A View on the Stour*, hang in prestigious art galleries around the world.

Questions

What makes Constable's paintings special?

Though he is remembered for his landscapes, it is his attention to detail that makes Constable's work so special. In paintings such as *Hampstead Heath, Looking Towards Harrow* or *Study of Clouds at Hampstead*, he captures the movement of the clouds and the changing weather. In *Rainstorm off the Coast at Brighton* or *Chain Pier, Brighton*, his bold brush strokes and use of flecks of white and touches of red bring the waves of the sea to life.

> 'It is an image of perfect peace (*The Haywain*), with the far meadows bathed in sunlight and the trees just beginning to lose their summer green. Constable actually lived in a world that was changing rapidly, rather like our own world, and he is looking back with sadness and love, with nostalgia.'
>
> *My Favourite Things: 75 Works of Art From Around the World* by Sister Wendy (Harry N. Abrams, 1999)

What inspired Constable?

Nature was Constable's greatest inspiration. In his paintings he attempted to show nature with all its beauty and changes. This doesn't sound groundbreaking to us but until the nineteenth century many artists only painted landscapes as backdrops and they were not very realistic.

Other Works to See

The White Horse – Frick Collection, New York
The Cornfield and *The Haywain* – National Gallery, London
View on the Stour and *Salisbury Cathedral* – Victoria and Albert Museum, London
Hampstead Heath, Looking Towards Harrow and *Rainstorm off the Coast at Brighton* – Royal Academy of Arts, London

weblinks

For more information about Constable, go to
www.waylinks.co.uk/fav/artist

Joseph M W Turner | 1775-1851

Often known as the 'painter of light', Turner is famous for his dramatic landscape paintings and watercolours. His **Romantic** style influenced the nineteenth century **Impressionist** painters.

The Grand Canal, Venice In this painting you can see how Turner magically captures the play of light on the water, the skyline and the buildings.

Early Years

Turner was born in London in 1775. He lost his mother when he was young and was mainly brought up by his father. With little money to fund schooling Turner's father educated his son. Turner soon showed a talent for drawing. At 14 he enrolled at the Royal Academy Schools and the following year he began to exhibit his work. At 18 he had his own studio and toured England and Wales making architectural drawings. By the time he was in his mid-twenties he was working with watercolour painter Thomas Girtin and making a good living.

Turner was a loner who liked to travel. Some of his most famous paintings are of the Italian city of Venice. He was so intrigued by the city, that he painted and sketched it more than 600 times. One of his most popular paintings is *The Grand Canal, Venice* from 1835.

Later Life

Turner never married and he didn't have many friends. He hated selling any of his painting but when he died in 1851 he gave 300 paintings and 20,000 watercolours and sketches to the English nation. He also requested that his large fortune be used to help struggling artists.

'Introduced today to the man that beyond all doubt is the greatest of the age; greatest in every faculty of the imagination, in every branch of scenic knowledge; at one the painter and the poet of the day.'

The author and art critic John Ruskin on his first meeting with J M W Turner
Turner in the Tate Collection by David Blayney Brown (Tate, 2002)

Questions

How did Turner inspire the Impressionist painters?

As he grew older, Turner's use of light and colour became more dramatic. In paintings like *Snowstorm* or *The Slave Ship* he doesn't always attempt to use realistic colours. Sometimes he uses colours that express his feelings or capture sensations. It was this break with tradition that inspired the Impressionists. They too allowed their own 'impression' of a scene to take over how they painted it.

What inspired Turner?

Turner put emotion into his work by adapting colour and light to reflect his own mood. In the painting *Rain, Steam and Speed* he seems to express his fear at the coming of the steam train. He does this using a blur of streaks and whirls that look like rain, steam and speed. Out of this confusion of brush strokes a train appears to hurtle out of the picture. The train is black and looks almost sinister.

Other Works to See

Most of Turner's works, including *Snowstorm* are on display at the Tate Gallery, London
Rain Steam and Speed – National Gallery, London
The Slave Ship – Museum of Fine Art, Boston
Grand Canal, Venice – Metropolitan Museum of Art, New York

'I have fortunately met with a good-tempered, funny, little elderly man... He is continually popping his head out of the window to sketch whatever strikes his fancy, and became quite angry because the conductor would not wait whilst he took a sunrise view of Macerata.'

A fellow traveller writes about J M W Turner as they travel in Italy
Turner by Graham Reynolds (Thames and Hudson, 1997)

weblinks

For more information about J M W Turner, go to
www.waylinks.co.uk/fav/artist

Rembrandt 1606-1669

When looking at the portraits of Rembrandt Harmensz van Rijn we come face-to-face with real people. Rembrandt did much more than paint what people looked like; he captured their personality and their feelings as well.

Early Years

Born in 1606 in Leiden, Holland, Rembrandt went on to become the greatest European artist of his day. The son of a rich miller, he learned how to paint when he was apprenticed to two different artists. Later, he moved to Amsterdam for six months after which he returned to his hometown to establish himself as a painter and to take on pupils.

By the age of 22 Rembrandt's portraits were attracting lots of attention and he received many commissions. In 1631 he was back in Amsterdam. He was now well known and made a good living painting the rich and important citizens of the city. He also painted biblical or mythological scenes and landscapes.

The Military Company of Captain Frans Banning Cocq (also known as 'The Night Watch') This work was a new way of painting a group of people. Instead of a still pose the guards are in motion and it looks as if they are about to march off the canvas.

In 1634 Rembrandt married Saskia van Ulenburgh, the beautiful daughter of a well-

'Very meticulous connoisseurs and amateurs of art...are disconcerted by his manner of painting and find themselves at a loss: unable to discover how his pictures are made...even the painter had no clear understanding of how it was done.'

German artist Eduard Kolloff
Historisches Taschenbuch, ed. Friedrich Raumer, 3rd series, Vol V, Liepzig 1854

connected family of Dutch art dealers. Saskia was the model for many of his paintings and sketches. Between 1635 and 1641 Saskia gave birth to four children but only their son Titus survived.

Later Life

When Saskia died in 1642 Rembrandt threw himself into his work. That year he painted possibly his most famous painting, *The Military Company of Captain Frans Banning Cocq* (also known as 'The Night Watch'). It is extraordinary because he has painted a group of people in a dramatic pose in a way that brings action and movement to the scene. The painting works as a whole because of the way Rembrandt has used dark and light. The contrasting shadows create atmosphere and drama.

Rembrandt found love again with his housekeeper and together they had a daughter, Cornelia. Though he did well as an artist he spent too much on his precious art collection and he became bankrupt in 1656. He continued to live and work in Amsterdam until his death in 1669.

Questions

Why are Rembrandt's self-portraits so interesting?

Rembrandt produced an enormous amount of work during his lifetime. He created about 600 paintings, 300 etchings and 2,000 drawings. Of these paintings at least 60 are self-portraits. Rembrandt painted himself at least once a year and the portraits span his whole lifetime. Each portrait seems to show a slightly different person. We see the changes, not always flattering, that time and experience can have upon one man.

Why is Rembrandt's style a mystery?

Many people agree that Rembrandt's special quality was his ability to see people for what they were. He had his own distinctive way of painting but the mystery is why it worked so well. Unlike many artists Rembrandt did not draw the subjects of his portraits or paintings on the canvas before he began work. He also applied light paint on top of dark paint, then built up the lightness by caking on more layers of paint. This is an unusual way of painting but it worked for Rembrandt.

'He observed himself in a mirror with complete sincerity... This is the face of a real human being. There is no trace of pose, no trace of vanity, just the penetrating gaze of the painter who scrutinizes his own features, ever ready to learn more and more about...the human face.'

The Story of Art by E. H. Gombrich (Phaidon, 1995)

Other Works to See

The Military Company of Captain Frans Banning Cocq – Rijksmuseum, Amsterdam
The Feast of Belshazzar – National Gallery, London
Self Portrait (1640) – National Gallery, London

weblinks

For more information about Rembrandt, go to
www.waylinks.co.uk/fav/artist

Édouard Manet | 1832-1883

Édouard Manet was born to an aristocratic family in Paris in 1832. As a boy his uncle regularly took him to the famous museum of art, the Louvre, in Paris.

Luncheon on the Grass (Déjeuner sur l'herbe) This important painting is now recognized as a major influence on **Impressionism**.

Early Years

Manet was well educated and his family expected him to become a lawyer or naval officer. Instead, when he turned 18, he began studying under the artist Thomas Couture. Manet appreciated the work of great painters in history but he had ideas of his own. He chose to look around him at the world he saw on his doorstep – Paris, an exciting modern city that was the centre of the art world.

In 1861 Manet's painting *The Spanish Guitar* was one of the most talked about paintings at the exhibition at the Salon, in Paris. Two years later, in 1863, his painting *Luncheon on the Grass* (*Déjeuner sur l'herbe*) was shown at the Salon but this time his work was condemned for showing a nude woman.

Later Life

The year 1863 wasn't all bad news. That year Manet married his long-term companion, the pianist Suzanne Leenhoff.

Manet became good friends with the Impressionists. They respected him for fighting against the more realistic way of painting, in his changes from dark to light and the shifts in focus he used to create a blurred effect. In turn, Manet was influenced by their modern techniques.

He painted his last great masterpiece, *Un Bar aux Folies-Bergères*, in 1881. He died in 1883.

'This war of daggers has done me a great deal of harm... But it was also a stimulus for me. I would not wish any painter praise and flattery from the very start. That would mean destruction of his personality.'

Manet on the criticism he received for *Luncheon on the Grass*.
Manet by Pierre Courthion (Harry N. Abrams Inc, 1984)

Questions

Why was everyone so shocked by *Luncheon on the Grass*?

In the painting the woman sitting on a picnic blanket is nude. The gentlemen alongside her are fully dressed. Art critics and the general public joined together in outrage. Why would a modern woman be just sitting there without any clothes? The artists of the past painted nudes too but they were women from classical stories or mythology. Not only did people find the painting vulgar but they questioned the use of light and shade and said that the painting appeared unfinished.

What is so special about *A Bar at the Folies-Bergères?*

In this painting Manet has captured so much detail that it is almost possible to imagine you are at the bar. You can nearly hear the bottles and glasses clinking as they sit on the bar top.

Other Works to See

Luncheon on the Grass – Musée d'Orsay, Paris
A Bar at the Folies-Bergères – Courtauld Institute Gallery, London
Music in the Tuileries – National Gallery, London

'Although he painted from life Manet did not by any means copy it. I realized his great gift was for simplification. He began to build up the woman's head but not by the means that nature offered him. Everything was concentrated: the tones were lighter, the colours brighter...The whole formed a light and tender harmony.'

A journalist describes watching Manet work
Manet by Pierre Courthion
(Harry N. Abrams Inc, 1984)

weblinks

For more information about Manet, go to
www.waylinks.co.uk/fav/artist

Pierre Auguste Renoir | 1841-1919

The paintings of the French nineteenth-century **Impressionist** artist Pierre-Auguste Renoir are among the most popular paintings in the world today.

Early Years
Renoir was born in Limoges, France in 1841. Soon afterwards his family moved to Paris. Renoir's career began at 13 when he worked in a porcelain factory hand-painting the delicate wares. In 1862 he joined the prestigious art school of Charles Gleyre. It was here that he met a group of young artists,

The Luncheon of the Boating Party
Renoir gives us a glimpse of what it must have been like to be at this meal on an enchanting sunny day in 1881.

including Claude Monet, Alfred Sisley and Jean-Frederic Bazille, with whom he later founded the Impressionist movement.

Throughout his early career Renoir struggled for acceptance. Then, in 1874, 1876, and again in 1877, he exhibited with the Impressionists.

His paintings were seen alongside painters like Camille Pissarro, considered the founder of the original Impressionists, and Paul Cézanne. It was Renoir's painting *Moulin de la Galette* that really caused controversy. This is now one of his most admired paintings but at the time people could not accept the way that Renoir used dabs of light paint to capture the sunlight filtering through the trees.

Later Life

In 1882 Renoir married Aline Charigot and together they had three boys. By now his works were becoming collectable. As he grew older he suffered from rheumatism and in 1903 he moved to the south of France to benefit from the warmer climate. His last years were spent in a wheelchair but he never stopped painting. When he died in 1919 he was famous throughout the world.

'I have no rules and no methods, anyone can look at my materials or watch how I paint.' Renoir

Artists in Profile: the Impressionists by Jeremy Wallis (Heinemann, 2002)

Questions

Why did Renoir's paintings cause such a stir?

Renoir did not follow the rules of the painters in the past. He didn't paint scenes from **mythology** or the Bible. He painted everyday images of ordinary people going about their life. He particularly liked painting scenes from Parisian suburban life; of people boating, dancing and enjoying themselves at picnics. He chose real subjects but did not try to make his paintings realistic. Instead he experimented with colour and brush strokes and created pictures that gave an 'impression' of what the scene looked like.

'Its (*The Luncheon of the Boating Party*) diaphanous brushwork beautifully catches the trembling leaves and shimmering water and quivering vibrations of air inundated with blazing summer light filtered through canvas awnings on to clean white linen and cut glass and soft human flesh.'

The World History of Art by Hugh Honour and John Fleming (Laurence King, 1995)

What makes Renoir's works special?

Renoir seems to capture moments in time very well as in his famous painting *The Luncheon of the Boating Party*. Many people also like Renoir because he painted flowers, beautiful natural scenes or pretty women as in his painting *The Umbrellas*. As he once said: 'Why shouldn't art be pretty? There are enough unpleasant things in the world.'

Other Works to See

Moulin de la Galette – Musée d'Orsay, Paris
The Luncheon of the Boating Party – Phillips Collection, Washington
The Umbrellas (Les Parapluies) – National Gallery, London
The Parisian – National Museum of Wales, Cardiff

weblinks

For more information about Renoir, go to
www.waylinks.co.uk/fav/artist

Auguste Rodin | 1840–1917

The French sculptor Auguste Rodin made sculptures that looked so real they might spring into life. He was the most influential sculptor of the nineteenth century.

Early Years

Rodin was born in Paris in 1840. He became interested in sculpture when he was just 15 but he made three attempts to join the famous École des Beaux-Arts and was turned down each time. To earn a living he worked as a decorator of stonework. In 1864 Rodin fell in love with Rose Beuret. In the same year he created his first major work, *The Man with the Broken Nose* (*L'Homme au Nez Cassé*).

Later he worked in Paris and Brussels as a sculptor's assistant. In 1875 he visited Italy and became fascinated by ancient Roman sculptures and the work of the **Renaissance** artist Michelangelo. In 1877 he toured around French cathedrals. Upon his return he set to work. The sculptures and works of art he had seen inspired him. He aimed to make his work natural, and gave his sculptures expression and movement. That year his sculpture, *The Age of Bronze* (*L'Âge d'Airain*), was exhibited at the Salon at the Royal Academy of Painting and Sculpture in Paris. It looked so lifelike

The Kiss (Le Baiser) In this sculpture the couple are kissing deeply and there is something very tender about the way they are holding each other.

that people accused Rodin of casting his sculpture from a real person.

Later Life

Though his work was controversial people had now heard about Rodin. In 1880 the government asked Rodin to create *The Gate of Hell* (*Porte de l'Enfer*), the pair of bronze doors for the Musée des Arts Décoratifs. Rodin spent the rest of his life producing the 186 figures that made up the door. Out of this major work came two of his best known statues, *The Kiss* (*Le Baiser*) and *The Thinker* (*Le Penseur*). Other major works include the monument *The Burghers of Calais* (*Les Bourgeois de Calais*).

Rodin died in 1917 at the age of 77. By this time he was famous throughout the world. The year before his death he gave all his works to the French nation.

> 'In short, I am a sculptor who, like you, asks only to make a masterpiece, if that be possible, and for whom the question of art takes precedence over all others.'
>
> Rodin to the editor of *La Patriote*, 1884
> *Rodin, the Shape of Genius* by Ruth Butler (Yale University Press, 1993)

Questions

Why is Rodin's work timeless?

Even though the couple in *The Kiss*, or subjects of many of his statues, could have been plucked from the modern world Rodin's style was still classical and inspired by ancient sculpture. At the same time Rodin created a contrast between the rough and the smooth areas of his sculptures which helped create an unfinished look. This added to the sense of movement.

> 'Despite everything, Rodin remains the giant, the titan of his century, the master of the young sculptor, and the procession of sculptors who enter into this career by passing under *The Gate of Hell* is not yet over… Once in a while the world yields up an inspired one. It may be a prophet, a soldier, a poet, an artist…'
>
> The French poet and art critic
> André Salmon
> *Rodin, the Shape of Genius* by Ruth Butler
> (Yale University Press, 1993)

Why is *The Kiss* important?

When *The Kiss* first appeared people couldn't help but be shocked by the passion they saw. At this time the French were used to historical subjects in the sculptures they saw, not people from the modern world.

Other Works to See

A Man and Woman – British Museum, London
L'Age D'Airain – Leeds City Art Gallery
Balzac – Tate, London
Brother and Sister – Tate, London
The Kiss – Tate, London
Today you can see casts of all Rodin's major works at the Musée Rodin in Paris. The museum is housed in the Hôtel Biron where Rodin actually lived when he stayed in Paris from 1908.

weblinks

For more information about Rodin, go to
www.waylinks.co.uk/fav/artist

Paul Cézanne | 1839–1906

The French **Post-Impressionist** painter Paul Cézanne was the inspiration for great artists like Pablo Picasso. Today, he is remembered as the 'father of modern art'.

Early Years

Cézanne was born in the town of Aix-en-Provence in Southern France in 1839. His childhood friend was the author Emile Zola. In 1861 Cézanne left his hometown to join Zola in Paris. By now he wanted to become an artist but it would be many years before he succeeded. Paris presented him with inspiration and disappointment. He found himself mixing with talented artists like Manet, Pissarro (probably his greatest influence) and Degas but he was turned down by the École des Beaux Arts. While in a fit of depression, he destroyed many of his early paintings.

Apples and Oranges (Pommes et Oranges) Unlike the Impressionists Cézanne was constantly concerned with the structure and weight of the objects he painted. The apples and oranges shown here look solid, almost as if you could reach out and pick one.

The year 1870 was a turning point. He met his future wife, Hortense Fiquet (although they didn't marry until 1886), and in his work he began to use the vibrant glowing colours for which he became famous. He divided his time between the countryside of Aix-en-

'We must not...be satisfied with retaining the beautiful formulas of our illustrious predecessors. Let us go forth to study beautiful nature...'

Taken from Cézanne's letter to Emile Bernard, July 1904
A World History of Art by Hugh Honour and John Fleming (Laurence King, 1995)

Provence where he enjoyed painting portraits, landscapes and still life, and Paris where he exhibited in 1874, 1876 and again in 1877 with the **Impressionists**. One of his most famous paintings from this time is *Man in a Straw Hat* (*L'Homme au Chapeau de Paille*).

Later Life

Cézanne could be a violent and moody man. In 1881 he fell out with Zola and he spent more and more time living alone in Aix. Of the hundreds of paintings he created, more than 200 were still lifes of everyday subjects such as fruit and vegetables. One of his most outstanding still life paintings is *Apples and Oranges* (*Pommes et Oranges*).

Cézanne didn't achieve much recognition or success until the 1890s. By this time he was an embittered man. He died of pneumonia in 1906.

Questions

Why is Cézanne called the 'father of modern art'?

In the 1870s Cézanne developed a new way of painting. He tried to break his subjects down into blocks of colour or straight lines. This way of looking at the world wasn't realistic but it was an exciting way of presenting his subjects. The artists Pablo Picasso and Georges Braques developed this idea of subjects being transformed into bold shapes. From 1908 they worked closely together producing paintings of subjects made up of cubes or geometric patterns. This way of painting became known as **Cubism**.

What makes Cézanne stand out?

Paris in the nineteenth century was the centre of the art world. Young artists from around the world came to the cultural capital. Cézanne only spent a short time in Paris, he preferred the quiet life in Aix. He wasn't part of any particular movement of art, though he did exhibit some of his work with the Impressionists. He stands out because he took everyday objects and injected them with colour and new life – nobody had done that before.

Other Works to See

Apples and Oranges – Louvre, Paris
Still Life with Water Jug, Rocky Landscape in Aix and *The Gardener* – Tate Modern, London
The Old Woman with Beads – The National Gallery, London
Man in a Straw Hat – Metropolitan Museum, New York

'When I first saw him, he looked like a cut-throat with large red eyeballs standing out from his head in a most ferocious manner, a rather fierce-looking pointed beard, quite grey, and an excited way of talking that positively made the dishes rattle.'

The Impressionist artist Mary Cassatt
Great Artists: Cézanne by David Speke
(TickTock Pubishing 1998)

weblinks

For more information about Cézanne, go to
www.waylinks.co.uk/fav/artist

Gustav Klimt 1862-1918

The Austrian painter and designer Gustav Klimt is famous for his paintings of women. He is remembered as one of the forerunners of the **Art Nouveau** movement.

Early Years

Klimt was born near the Austrian capital of Vienna in 1862. He came from a family of gold engravers but unfortunately they were not rich themselves. At 14 Klimt enrolled at the Vienna Public Art School. He did so well that while he was still a student he was commissioned to decorate the stairway of the Burgtheatre in Vienna.

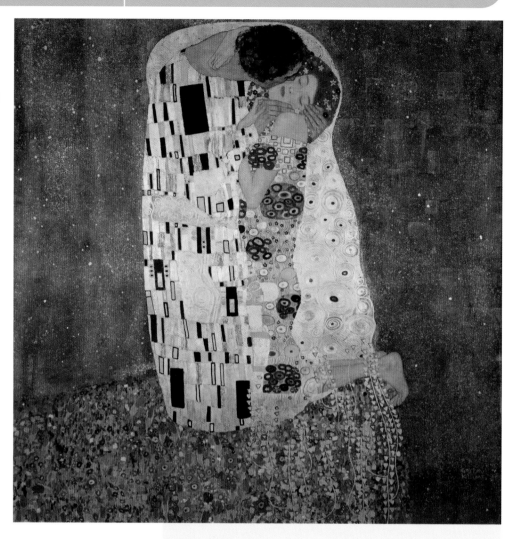

The Kiss Klimt's painting is very romantic and luxurious. The clothes are highly decorated with patterns.

In 1883, at the age of 21, Klimt launched a business designing decorative schemes. Together with his brother Ernst and another student, Franz Matsch, they were commissioned to paint murals for the lobby of the Museum of Art History. Even in his early projects Klimt was developing a unique style. In 1893 he was commissioned to produce paintings that represented the University of Vienna's faculties. Unfortunately, his murals

'I am convinced that I am not particularly interesting as a person…if anyone wants to find out about me – as an artist, the only capacity in which I am of any note – they should look carefully at my paintings and try to learn from them what I am and what I have tried to achieve.'

Klimt

were criticised for showing too much nudity. It was a criticism that followed him for the rest of his life.

Later Life

Klimt never worked on a public commission again. Instead, he dedicated himself to creating art that he believed in. The final years of the nineteenth century were an exciting time to live in Vienna. Groups of radical artists were inventing new techniques and exploring new ideas in art. From 1897 to 1903 Klimt was one of the leaders of the art scene, becoming founder and president of the Vienna Secession, a group of artists dedicated to avant-garde art. One of Klimt's most memorable projects from this time is *The Beethoven Frieze* that decorated the Secession Building in Vienna.

Klimt lived and worked in Vienna for the rest of his life. His most famous works include *Adele Bloch-Bauer* and *The Kiss*. He died in 1918 from a stroke.

Questions

What is the power of *The Kiss*?

In this work the couple are passionately embracing. Though the picture isn't realistic it expresses sensuality in a powerful and exciting way. However, it is the patterns and the rich gold that Klimt uses for the blanket over the lovers and throughout the whole painting that makes it so impressive.

Why are the works of Klimt still popular today?

Klimt's paintings are very much of their time, capturing the spirit of the Art-Nouveau movement. Yet, these pictures that were fashionable over one hundred years ago still look fresh and exciting today. Klimt manages to do this because his paintings look as if they represent another world. Sometimes they make you feel like you're stepping into a place of fairytales and make believe. His women are beautiful and relaxed. The gold, orange, purple, blue, pink and reds that he tended to use are deep and exotic.

'There is always a sensitive eye at work, seeking out the charms of womanhood in each individual. Some enchanting feature resides in every woman, reveals itself in every woman in some sign, and Klimt always discovers it – even in one less attractive. It might be an eye, which he makes shine in such a way that the whole picture seems to be all eye; or a dry, thirsty mouth, which he paints with such eloquence that all else vanishes besides the mouth, or it is the line of her body, the gesture of her hands or her hair.'

Felix Salten, *Geisterder Zeit Erlebnisse*, Vienne-Leipzig, 1924
Art Nouveau by Gabriele Fahr-Becker (Konemann, 1997)

Other Works to See

The Kiss – Belvedere Gallery, Vienna
Beethoven Frieze – Secession Building, Vienna
The Portrait of Hermine Gallia – Tate Modern, London

For more information about Klimt, go to
www.waylinks.co.uk/fav/artist

Mary Cassatt | 1844-1926

In the nineteenth century Mary Cassatt became the only American to be welcomed into the **Impressionist** movement. This was more remarkable because she was a woman.

Early Years

Cassatt was born into a wealthy family of stockbrokers in Pennsylvania, USA in 1844. When she was 16 she studied at the Pennsylvania Academy of Fine Arts. After

A Goodnight Hug Some of Cassatt's work is so touching and intimate that it is almost as if we are privileged to share the moment.

college she went to France to paint and attend art classes. In 1868 her painting *The Mandolin Player* was exhibited at the Salon, at the Royal Academy of Painting and Sculpture in Paris.

'I accepted with joy. Now I could work with absolute independence without considering the opinion of a jury... I took leave of conventional art. I began to live.'

Cassatt upon being asked to exhibit with the Impressionists.

From 1874 Cassatt made Paris her permanent home and in 1877 she was joined by her parents and sister, Lydia. Soon afterwards she became friends with the Impressionist painter Degas. From 1877 to 1881, and again in 1886, she was invited to exhibit her works with the Impressionists. At this time serious art was considered to be a male pursuit so Cassatt was deeply honoured.

Cassatt's life was dogged by personal loss. Her sister Lydia died in 1882, she lost her father in 1891 and her mother died in 1895. Though she never married herself, or had children of her own, she was close to her family and friends' children and enjoyed painting them.

She painted *The Bath* in 1893, the year of her first solo show in Paris. As well as oil painting she experimented with printing, copying the Japanese method of using wooden blocks.

Later Life

For many years Cassatt was well known in France but largely ignored by her native America, though she was commissioned in 1893 to create a mural for the International Exposition in Chicago. In 1910 she was finally made a member of the National Academy of Design in New York. Ill-health and failing eyesight forced her to give up painting in 1914 and she died in 1926. Today, her paintings are highly prized by American collectors.

Questions

Why is Cassatt different to the other Impressionists?

Like her fellow Impressionists Cassatt used her paintings to capture one brief moment. However, Cassatt painted domestic scenes, especially with women or children. In *A Goodnight Hug* we see a tender moment between a mother and a child as they hug before bedtime.

Did Cassatt ever paint men?

Cassatt rarely painted men but when she did, it was with the same sensitivity that she painted women and children. In *Portrait of Alexander J. Cassatt* and *His Son Robert Kelso Cassatt* painted her brother with his son. She captures the strong bond between father and son by showing them sitting together in an armchair. Though they appear stiff and not quite as tender as the women she paints, she manages to convey their underlying closeness.

Other Works to See

The Bath – Art Institute of Chicago
The Child's Caress – Honolulu Academy of Art, Hawaii
Portrait of a Lady – National Gallery of Art, Washington
Portrait of a Little Girl – National Gallery of Art, Washington
Autumn – Musée du Petit Palais, Paris

'It is real. There is someone who feels as I do.'
Degas upon first seeing Cassatt's paintings
Mary Cassatt by Maria Gostantino
(Grange Books, 1995)

weblinks

For more information about Cassatt, go to
www.waylinks.co.uk/fav/artist

Other favourite classic artists

There are many more paintings by classic artists for you to see and get to know. Here are a few more introductions:

Vincent Willem Van Gogh (1853-1890)

The Dutch painter Van Gogh is famous for his paintings of objects or scenes from everyday life. Some of his most famous paintings include *Sunflowers, The Chair and the Pipe* and *Van Gogh's Room at Arles*. All of these pictures are painted in vibrant colours with thick brush strokes.

Van Gogh was born in Groot-Zundert in Holland. He was a self-taught artist who found inspiration when he moved to Arles in the Provençal region of France. As well as the beautiful landscape he painted still life and portraits. He became great friends with the artist Paul Gauguin and invited him to stay with him in Arles. When the artists quarrelled Van Gogh sliced off part of his own ear (he painted a self-portrait with a bandage on his ear). He was later placed in an asylum but he committed suicide by shooting himself in 1890. At the time of his death he had only sold one of his paintings.

Pablo Picasso (1881-1973)

The Spanish painter Picasso moved to Paris when he was still a teenager. He lived in France until his death. He experimented with many kinds of painting techniques as well as pottery, sculpture and set design for the ballet. He is often cited as the most inspirational artist of the twentieth century.

In his early years in Paris, Picasso painted many street scenes. To express the misery he saw he used shades of blue paint. Soon after his Blue Period he became inspired by acrobats and circus performers and painted them using shades of red, pink and brown. One of Picasso's most groundbreaking works is called *Les Demoiselles d'Avignon*. In this picture he painted a group of women. Their bodies are broken up into strange angular shapes and their faces look like African masks. When people saw the painting in 1907 they were terribly shocked. In fact, this painting became the inspiration for a new movement in art called **Cubism**.

Edgar Degas (1834-1917)

The French painter and sculptor Edgar Degas was born in Paris in 1834 and studied art at the École des Beaux-Arts. After his studies he visited Italy where he sought inspiration from the **Renaissance** artists and painted in the classical style. All this changed on his return to Paris when he met the French painter Manet and other **Impressionist** painters. He exhibited with the Impressionists from 1877 to 1881 and again in 1886, becoming one of the most famous members of the group.

Among Degas' better known pictures are those of ballerinas, such as *Rehearsal of the Ballet, Dancer at the Bar* and *Dancer Lacing her Shoe*. As he grew older his eyesight began to fail and he turned to sculpture. One of his most famous pieces is the sculpture *The Little Dancer*.

Michelangelo Buonarroti (1475-1564)

The Italian sculptor, painter, architect and poet Michelangelo is possibly the best known **Renaissance** artist. He was born in the Italian region of Tuscany in the fifteenth century. He spent his early years in Florence where he became an apprentice painter.

In 1492 Michelangelo was living in Bologna. During his three years there he made the beautiful marble sculpture of *Cupid*. His talents did not go unnoticed and he was called to Rome where he created his famous works, *Bacchus* and *Pieta*. Four years later he was back in Florence and in 1501 began work on his famous marble statue *David*.

Michelangelo was also a dedicated painter. Perhaps his most magnificent work is the decoration of the ceiling of the Sistine Chapel in Rome, which he undertook between 1508 and 1512. In a series of nine frescoes he shows his interpretation of the *Creation of the World* and of *Man, the Fall and the Flood*. Michelangelo returned to the Sistine Chapel from 1535 to 1541 to paint *The Last Judgement*.

Michelangelo Merisi da Caravaggio (1573-1610)

The Italian painter Caravaggio lived a life as bold and adventurous as his paintings. Born near Milan in 1573, he moved to Rome when he was a teenager. Successful by the time he was 20, his early commissions included *The Life of Saint Matthew* at the Contarelli Chapel of the Church of San Luigi dei Francese in Rome. Even in this early work he established his own distinct style. The figures appear realistic as they are based on sketches of real life models. (Many of these models were from Rome's low-life.) This kind of realism was groundbreaking but it was also controversial. People didn't like seeing biblical characters portrayed in a less than perfect way.

Caravaggio remained in Rome until 1606 but he was forced to flee the city when he murdered a man in a fight. For the rest of his life he moved between Naples, Sicily and Malta. He died from fever in 1610. His significant works include *Fruit Basket* and *Salome*.

Francisco José de Goya y Lucientes (1746-1828)

Goya is sometimes called the first of the modern artists. He influenced great painters like Picasso. Born in the village of Feundetodos in Spain in 1775, Goya himself was influenced by the great Dutch painter Rembrandt and the Spanish painter Velázquez.

Goya began his career painting tapestry cartoons at his local cathedral. In later years he became court painter to King Charles IV of Spain. His paintings of the royal Spanish family were so true to life that they appear totally unflattering. In a series of etchings called *Los Caprichos* he made fun of the royal court. Other famous works from this time include the portraits of a woman, possibly the Duchess of Alba: *The Naked Maja* and *The Clothed Maja* which at the time were criticized for being too erotic. Later, his series of etchings called *The Disasters of War* showed the full horror of the Napoleonic War.

Glossary

Romanticism/Romantic
An early 19th century movement in art in which painters expressed themselves in an individual and imaginative way. There was an almost dreamlike quality to Romantic paintings.

Impressionism/Impressionist
A late 19th century movement in art which was concerned with the painting of real-life subjects. Impressionists painted their first 'impression' of what they saw using rapid, broken brushstrokes and strong, clear colours to show the effect of light.

Post-Impressionism/Post-Impressionist
A late 19th century movement in art which was concerned with form and structure. Unlike the Impressionists, the Post-Impressionists were not interested in painting subjects in a naturalistic way.

Cubism/Cubist
An early 20th century movement in art in which painters sought to represent objects as they are known rather than as they appear. Instead of using a single fixed viewpoint, they represented a subject from a number of different angles simultaneously.

Art Nouveau (New Art)
A movement in art that started in the late 19th century and continued until about 1910. The movement was influenced by the past, but Art Nouveau paintings had a contemporary, highly decorative style.

Renaissance (Rebirth)
The intellectual movement that took place in European culture from the 14th century to the 16th century. It was a time of brilliant artistic achievement, in which painters were concerned with the naturalistic representation of a subject based on classical values.

Index

Artists, American 20-21
        Austrian 18-19
        Dutch 8-9, 22
        English 4-5, 6-7
        French 10-11, 12-13, 14-15,
            16-17
        Italian 23
        Spanish 22, 23

Art Nouveau 18, 19
Avant Garde 19

Bible 13, 23

Carvaggio 23
Cassatt, Mary 20-21
Cézanne, Paul 16-17
Constable, John 4-5
Cubism 17, 22

Degas, Edgar 16, 21, 22

Etchings 9, 23

Goya 23

Impressionists 6, 7, 11, 12-13, 17,
            21, 22

Klimt, Gustav 18-19

Landscape painting 4, 6, 8, 17
Light 7, 9, 11, 13
Louvre, Paris 10

Manet, Édouard 10-11, 16
Michelangelo 14, 22,
Mythology 8, 13

Nature 5
Nudes 11, 19

Picasso, Pablo 17, 22, 23
Pissarro, Camille 13, 16
Portraits 8, 9, 16, 22, 23
Post-Impressionist 16-17

Rembrandt 8-9
Renaissance 14, 22, 23
Renoir, Pierre Auguste 12-13
Rodin, Auguste 14-15
Romantic 6

Salon, Paris 11, 14, 20
Sculpture 14-15
Self-portraits 9
Sistine Chapel 23
Still life 16, 22

Turner J M W 6-7

Van Gogh 22